GOD'S LITTLE BOOK OF

LITTLE BOOKS
FOR MOMS

GUARANTEES

HEATHER KOPP

Multnomah® Publishers *Sisters, Oregon*

GOD'S LITTLE BOOK OF GUARANTEES FOR MOMS
published by Multnomah Publishers, Inc.
Published in association with the literary agency of Ann Spangler and Associates,
1420 Pontiac Road, S.E., Grand Rapids, Michigan 49506

© 2002 by Heather Kopp
International Standard Book Number: 1-59052-023-8

Cover image by Getty Images

Unless otherwise indicated, Scripture quotations are the author's own paraphrase.
Other Scripture quotations: *The Holy Bible,* New King James Version (NKJV)
© 1984 by Thomas Nelson, Inc.
The Holy Bible, New International Version (NIV)
© 1973, 1978, 1984 by International Bible Society,
used by permission of Zondervan Publishing House

Multnomah is a trademark of Multnomah Publishers, Inc.,
and is registered in the U.S. Patent and Trademark Office.
The colophon is a trademark of Multnomah Publishers, Inc.

Printed in the United States of America

For information:
MULTNOMAH PUBLISHERS, INC. • P.O. BOX 1720 • SISTERS, OR 97759

Library of Congress Cataloging-in-Publication Data

Kopp, Heather Harpham, 1964–
   God's little book of guarantees for moms / by Heather Kopp.
      p. cm.
   ISBN 1-59052-023-8 (pbk.)
   1. Mothers—Prayer-books and devotions—English. 2. God—Promises—
Prayer-books and devotions—English.   I. Title.
      BV4847 .K67 2002
      242'.6341—dc21

                                        2002006757

02 03 04 05 06 07 08—10 9 8 7 6 5 4 3 2 1 0

Table of Contents

One

God's

Guarantees

about His

Provision for

Your Child

God Guarantees

YOUR CHILD HAS ALL HE NEEDS TO LIVE A HOLY LIFE

When your child accepts and exhibits My grace, he makes evident that righteousness has taken hold—and how rich this is! It means he has the tools, inspiration, and courage to go after holiness—all he will ever need for a meaningful and satisfying spiritual life. Through one man came death to all, but through one man, My Son, came life. Your sons and daughters can know this abundance. I guarantee it to those who seek it.

FROM ROMANS 5:17–18

WARRANTY NOTES: NO SHOPPING NECESSARY FOR THIS SCHOOL TERM—GOD PROVIDES!

Dear God, I'm so grateful that You minister to my child's spirit. I commit him to Your care today and to the provision only You can manage.

Amen.

I WILL GIVE YOUR CHILD PLEASURE

Show your children, especially if they have many material resources, how to put their hope in Me; I am the only safe place for their hearts' longings. As you know, money is uncertain. But I'm steadfast, abounding in love, full of goodwill. I'll richly provide your children all good things to enjoy.

FROM 1 TIMOTHY 6:17

WARRANTY NOTES: WHY LOOK ANYWHERE BUT TO THE CREATOR OF PLEASURE FOR ITS SUPPLY?

Dear God,
Beyond the spiritual satisfaction I feel when I serve You,
I also know deep earthly enjoyment.
You are kind and giving, and I feel Your pleasure when
I'm delighting in one of Your gifts.
Thank You for this bountiful blessing.
Amen.

I PROVIDE ONLY
GOOD THINGS

My gifts to your children will always be just that: gifts. No tricks, no scary surprises—in short, no snakes when they ask for fish. A good father offers only nourishment, not danger or diminishment. Trust Me to be better than the best dad you can think of—you can rely on Me to do this.

FROM MATTHEW 7:9–11

WARRANTY NOTES: FATHER—THE HEAVENLY ONE, THAT IS—KNOWS BEST. TRUST HIM!

Dear God,
A child can never have too many fathers—especially if one is perfect! I'm grateful for the parenting You provide. I know that You make up for my failures as well as those of my kids' dad. No one is perfect but You, and I trust You to give good things to my children.
Amen.

God Guarantees

I NEVER CHANGE

When it comes to your child's provision (or yours), I'm no shifting shadow. I'm solid, dependable, and as sure as the sunrise. Though many things that I created change, I remain steadfast— how could you rely on Me otherwise? I promise you and your family that I, the Father of the heavenly lights, provide flawless gifts—faithfully.

FROM JAMES 1:17

WARRANTY NOTES: WHO NEEDS A SHIFTY SUPPLIER? GOD IS SO GOOD!

Dear God,
Your provision is something I am learning to rely on,
and I want to teach my children to do the same.
You have never let me down;
You have never stood me up.
This is a rare quality, and I thank You for
expressing it to my family.
Amen.

God Guarantees

I AM THE LORD
OF THE HARVEST

Can a garden grow without water? Can a flower bloom without sun? In order for a harvest to occur, soil, weather, and seed must collaborate in perfect unison. So it is with your children. They can accomplish all they're meant to accomplish—with My help. We must operate in flawless harmony. I promise to give what is good so this can happen. I want to see wonderful things growing in your child's life as much as you do!

FROM PSALM 85:12

WARRANTY NOTES: YOU CAN PLANT AND WATER—BUT ONLY GOD CAN MAKE IT GROW.

Dear God,
I am eager to see what You do with
this child I give to You. May I be a faithful
cultivator and cooperate with Your work in his life.
Amen.

God Guarantees

I SUSTAIN MY PEOPLE

I am aware of your child's every need, from the most basic—food, clothing, shelter—to the intangible needs he rarely expresses aloud—love, encouragement, confidence. I provide all of these to those who fear Me and embrace the holiness of My ways. I remember constantly My commitment to you and your family, and I sustain more than stomachs. I promise to do this forever for your child, who is also My child.

FROM PSALM 111:5

WARRANTY NOTES: EVEN THOSE THINGS THAT ARE HARD TO COME BY, GOD HAS IN ABUNDANT SUPPLY. AREN'T YOU GLAD HE SHARES?

Dear God, I have known Your provision on many levels—physical, spiritual, emotional—and I praise You for being faithful to me. Remind me to remind my children where all sustenance really comes from and that our Supplier must love us a lot to give so freely.

Amen.

God Guarantees

I GIVE YOUR CHILD HOPE

Trust the designer: The life I have planned for your God-following child is one of joy! Righteous people shouldn't look for anything less. While the wicked hope in vain, the righteous enjoy rich and satisfying expectations—because they hope for the right things.

FROM PROVERBS 10:28

WARRANTY NOTES: A HOPE WELL AIMED IS A HOPE SUSTAINED.

Dear God,
I can think of no better promise:
eternal hope, ultimate joy.
Thank You for offering these things to
the young as well as the old.
Because of You, my children have
much to look forward to.
Amen.

God Guarantees

I PROVIDE MINISTRY OPPORTUNITIES FOR YOUR CHILDREN

"The light of the righteous shines brightly" (NIV). One candle can dispel much darkness. Know that the light your children exude by righteous living will affect others—I have ordained it. I promise to use them in my service as they "glow" with obedience!

FROM PROVERBS 13:9

WARRANTY NOTES: KEEP THAT FAITH SHINY— AND DON'T FORGET TO POLISH YOUR KIDS' FAITH TOO.

Dear God,
Please shine through us, both mother and child.
We want others to know You as Lord,
as Provider, as King, and as Friend.
Amen.

I PROVIDE FOR YOUR CHILD THAT HE MAY PROVIDE FOR OTHERS

One of the ways grace will show up in your child's life is through his concern for those who have less than he does. I provide for him—both the grace that opens his eyes as well as the material goods he needs—so that he can provide for others. Know that I intend wealth for sharing and that I promise to bless the giver.

FROM PROVERBS 29:7

WARRANTY NOTES: THERE'S NO SUCH THING AS A SELFISH SAINT.

Dear God,
Make my child see those he can help in any way—
with a helping hand, a friendly word, a shared cookie.
I want him to learn to give in the same abundance
with which he has received.
Amen.

God Guarantees

I PROVIDE THE SMALL WITH GREAT WISDOM

I have given even the ant enough intelligence to store its food in summer and harvest it in fall. Size is irrelevant to capacity when it comes to wisdom. Even your young child can learn and rehearse common sense and discernment. I promise to make these available to every child who desires them—and to bless their practice.

FROM PROVERBS 6:6–8

WARRANTY NOTES: ANTS MAY BE PUNY IN SIZE, BUT THEY HUMBLE US WITH THEIR GOOD SENSE. MAY WE LIVE AS SMART!

Dear God,
Give me the wisdom of the ant.
I want to model good sense—God sense—
to my children and bless You with it as well.
Amen.

Two

God's

Guarantees

about His

Strength

God Guarantees

YOUR WEAKNESS IS
MY OPPORTUNITY

Who knows more than I do how you are formed?
I created people from dust! Your days on the earth
are brief and fragile, but know that My love is with
you every step of the way. I promise to fill in the
gaps when your own strength is spent.

FROM PSALM 103:15–17

WARRANTY NOTES: WE NEVER SURPRISE GOD
WITH OUR WEAKNESS; RATHER, WE CREATE
OPPORTUNITIES FOR HIM TO SHOW HIS
POWER THROUGH US. HE PROMISES TO
KEEP REFILLING US. FOR HOW LONG? THE
PSALMIST SAYS "FROM EVERLASTING TO
EVERLASTING" (NKJV).

*Dear God, today my strength is small. Will You inspire
me with Your power to accomplish all that You have
assigned me as a mother this day? I want to give You
glory, which I can do only through Your strength.*
Amen.

RENEWAL COMES
FROM REST

Are you exhausted? Feeble? Dragging? Do you carry things too heavy for your human frame, things such as your child's lack of friends, your family's financial well-being, or your own weak faith? Come to Me. Learn a better way from Me, your gentle teacher. Strength will rise from the rest you give your soul by trusting in Me.

FROM MATTHEW 11:28–29

WARRANTY NOTES: A RUBBER BAND, STRETCHED TOO FAR, WILL ALWAYS BREAK. SO WILL A HUMAN BEING.

Dear God, thank You for offering to carry my burdens. Thank You for inviting me to rest. Sometimes I feel guilty for needing replenishment, but I know the result if I don't care for myself: I won't be able to care for anyone else, especially my family.
Amen.

God Guarantees

I AM THE SOURCE OF INNER STRENGTH

Your deep strength of character comes not from eating and sleeping and exercising; it comes from trusting! As you release your deficiencies to Me, your heart will leap for joy and you will find relief and praise. You will have all the strength you need.

FROM PSALM 28:7

WARRANTY NOTES: WE DEVELOP A SOLID INNER CORE WHEN WE PUT OUR FAITH IN GOD—WE BECOME UNSHAKABLE, UNBREAKABLE, UNSTOPPABLE.

Dear God,
I want to be a believer from the inside out.
Help me to trust You more, love You more,
and praise You more, as a mom and as a disciple.
Amen.

I WILL EMPOWER
YOUR GOOD WORKS

Because of love and for the sake of grace, my Son and I created for you a lasting encouragement and a powerful hope—eternal salvation! We will take this gift a step further: Here on earth we will enliven your hearts and inspire your every wise word and good deed. As a mom, you can expect amazing ideas, extra energy, and endless love for those in your care.

FROM 2 THESSALONIANS 2:16–17

WARRANTY NOTES: WILL THE GOD WHO GAVE US JESUS KEEP FROM US ANYTHING ELSE WE NEED?

Dear God, I praise You for Your love and grace, encouragement and hope. I ask for the courage to speak each word and to act upon each assignment You give me as a mother, wife, friend, sister, daughter, and neighbor. Please "build" many great works through me.
Amen.

God Guarantees

I Want "Clinging" Souls

Because I am your help, you can find a song even in the darkness of a child's illness, school struggles, or faithless friends. Safety abides in the shadow of My wings. As you hold on to Me, My right hand upholds you—and your child.

FROM PSALM 63:7–8

Warranty Notes: It's a wonderful exchange: weakness for strength, silence for song. As we cling to God, He offers us all the support we need.

Dear God,
I feel that I'm failing as a mom today.
My soul is ready to cling—will You help me?
Amen.

God Guarantees

My Power Is Close at Hand

I have called you to a life of power, a life that reflects the same astonishing power that raised My Son from the dead. And Jesus not only rose from an earthly grave; He now sits at My right hand in heavenly heights! There He exercises, on your behalf, ultimate rule and authority, strength and domination, not just today but also tomorrow— and every tomorrow to come. Rest assured that His power is yours for the asking.

FROM EPHESIANS 1:18–21

WARRANTY NOTES: WHAT DOES GOD'S POWER EXIST FOR? ALL GOOD PURPOSES—INCLUDING THOSE OF BEING A WISE AND GODLY MOM.

Dear God, I'm glad You are strong, for I am weak and worn out. Will you infuse me with Your power today so that I can accomplish every good thing You have assigned me? With Your help, I can do it.

Amen.

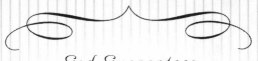

God Guarantees

Joy Is Like a Vitamin

You have already tapped the biggest blessing: Though you have not seen My Son, you love Him, embrace Him, and believe Him. The result? Joy—mind-blowing, praise-spouting joy! This is evidence that you are even now receiving the aim of your faith—your soul is saved. You can be certain that your joy will refresh you and those around you—especially your family.

FROM 1 PETER 1:7–9

WARRANTY NOTES: NEHEMIAH, ONE OF GOD'S FAITHFUL, REINVIGORATED THE ISRAELITES BY SAYING, "THE JOY OF THE LORD IS YOUR STRENGTH" (NEHEMIAH 8:10, NKJV). THIS IS TRUE FOR ALL OF THE LORD'S SERVANTS. CAN YOU ACCESS THIS WELLSPRING TODAY?

Dear God, thank You for an ever-flowing spring from which to draw. When my own current is low, thank You for refreshing me from Your perfect source. Fill me to overflowing, please!

Amen.

God Guarantees

My Eyes Are on You to Strengthen You

I'm keeping My eye on you. I know that your heart is fully Mine; therefore I welcome the sight of you serving your family, relishing your relationship with Me, and exuding the joy that comes from commitment. Rest assured that when need arises in your life, I will give you the strength you need because you love Me.

FROM 2 CHRONICLES 16:9

WARRANTY NOTES: DID YOU KNOW THAT EVERY GOOD THING YOU DO COUNTS? GOD IS KEEPING TRACK OF YOUR GODLY DEEDS, AND HE WILL REWARD EACH ONE.

Dear God, what a relief to know that You are eager to empower me, for I often feel utterly powerless to affect anyone for good. Of course! You are the source of good, so You are also the source of strength to accomplish it. I rest in that today.

Amen.

God Guarantees

I WON'T CALL
YOU WITHOUT
EMPOWERING YOU

Don't worry about your human frailties. If I call
you to speak, you will speak words I give you. If
you serve, you will do so with My strength, not
yours. I don't expect you to pull off *anything*—loving
your children perfectly, seeking Me faithfully,
or attending to friends' needs—without My help.
Ask and I'll give it—I promise!

FROM EPHESIANS 4:11–12

WARRANTY NOTES: AS A MOM, YOU KNOW
THAT NURTURING IS A FULL-TIME CALLING.
FORTUNATELY, YOU HAVE A FULL-TIME GOD.

Dear God, thank You for the calling You have for me
and for making me adequate for every situation You call
me to. Help me to model for my children that help is
always just a prayer away.
Amen.

God Guarantees

YOUR ACTIONS
GLORIFY ME

Think for a moment about those in your care. In the last twenty-four hours, whom did you comfort with a soft hug? Whom did you encourage by pointing out a skill? Whom did you strengthen with an appreciative glance or kind word? You can be certain that I am aware of every way you express My love to your family, and I celebrate your success!

FROM JOB 4:3–4

WARRANTY NOTES: HOW FORTUNATE THAT WE CAN GIVE GOD GLORY WITHOUT EVEN THINKING ABOUT IT!

Dear God, I want to honor You and exalt You in the midst of my family life, but I'm often so busy that I don't plan ways to do this. Thank You for noticing each effort, however clumsily made, to be a good mom—and daughter of God.

Amen.

Three

God's Guarantees about His Love for Your Child

God Guarantees

I WELCOME CHILDREN INTO MY ARMS AND MY KINGDOM

My Son rebuked the disciples for refusing to admit children to one of His gatherings. When people asked Him to lay hands on them and bless them— as you do now—He was and is more than willing. Children, you see, model exactly the kind of simple faith and courage I want to see in all My followers. I promise to welcome your child into My arms.

FROM MATTHEW 19:14

WARRANTY NOTES: IT'S ONE OF GOD'S BEST PARADOXES: CHILDREN TEACH ADULTS HOW TO APPROACH HIM—EAGERLY AND OPENLY.

Dear God, my life would be so much simpler if I remembered to come to You as a child comes to a father who loves her. Make me aware of the ways my children draw near to me and to You—let me learn from them.
Amen.

God Guarantees

I SAVOR
CHILDREN'S PRAISE

My Son didn't still the children who praised Him; rather, He celebrated them! I designed even these very young ones to offer Me worship and gladness, and I relish it. Know that whenever your child lifts his voice to Me, I will hear, I will smile, and I will bless. It is a worthy gift, no matter the size or age of the worshiper!

FROM MATTHEW 21:15–16

WARRANTY NOTES: PRAISE IS SWEET TO GOD'S EARS, WHOEVER GIVES IT.

Dear God,
Thank You for honoring my children's gifts of praise.
I want to teach them to glorify You
in all places and in all circumstances.
Help me, please, to teach by example.
Amen.

God Guarantees

ANGELS WATCH OVER YOUR CHILDREN

Your children are always in My sight. Therefore, honor them as My creations as I do—I have assigned angelic guardians to every one!

FROM MATTHEW 18:10–11

WARRANTY NOTES: WHAT A RELIEF TO KNOW THAT EVEN WHEN OUR CHILDREN ARE OUT OF OUR SIGHT, THEY ARE WITHIN GOD'S— AND HE CONSIDERS THEM WORTHY OF SUPERNATURAL PROTECTORS.

Dear God,
Thank You for caring for my children
in all the ways I can't.
I am unspeakably grateful for the
angels You have set around them.
As You watch over them today,
please remind them of Your special love and care.
Amen.

I LOVE YOUR CHILDREN

"Dear children"—that is how I think of My disciples. Why? Because those who follow Me express the same innocence, helplessness, and open affection as those young ones we treasure in families. I chose this term carefully. It reflects My lifelong commitment to and fatherly affection for all who bear My name. You can be certain that every child in My care—including yours—has a loving Father who seeks his success.

FROM 1 JOHN 3:1

WARRANTY NOTES: EARTHLY FATHERS FAIL, BUT YOUR HEAVENLY FATHER NEVER WILL.

Dear God,
I am grateful for Your perfect parental care,
especially because my own is so imperfect.
Today I lean on You and savor Your love for my
children, and watch for Your help in raising them well.
Amen.

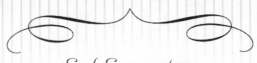

YOUR CHILDREN WILL
BE BLESSED BY YOUR
WISE LIVING

A pure man is a blameless man. No one can accuse him of evildoing; no one can take away his confidence; nothing can crumble his faith. Such a man passes My blessings to his children both by example and by experience. Know that your godly behavior will reward not only you but also your family.

FROM PROVERBS 20:7

WARRANTY NOTES: IT'S THE TRICKLE-DOWN EFFECT. YOUR GOOD CHOICES MEAN GOOD RESULTS FOR ALL WHO KNOW YOU, ESPECIALLY THOSE IN YOUR FAMILY. REMEMBER, THOUGH, THE TRICKLE IS ONLY AS PURE AS ITS SOURCE.

Dear God, I want to lead a righteous life, one that blesses You and my children. Please continue to lead me in Your light as I strive to serve You with all my heart.

Amen.

God Guarantees

YOUR CHILDREN ARE
A BOUNTIFUL GIFT

Children are not random occurrences in an unmanaged universe; they are a present designed especially by Me for you! I send them as rewards to those who serve Me. And they are more than delightful packages; they are tools in the hands of My workers. Believe that your children serve eternal purposes—that I want to bless you with them. You know My pleasure if you have many such blessings in your home.

FROM PSALM 127:3–5

WARRANTY NOTES: CHILDREN ARE AMAZING BUNDLES OF ENERGY AND KEY PLAYERS IN GOD'S KINGDOM. HAVE YOU DREAMED ABOUT HOW THEY WILL SERVE GOD AS THEY GROW?

Dear God, thank You for the "arrows" in my "quiver."
When I forget that these young people are gifts to me
and servants to You, remind me how special each one is.
Amen.

God Guarantees

YOUR CHILDREN CAN WALK WITH ME FROM A YOUNG AGE

I am every person's hope, from cradle to grave. Your own faith began when you were young and continues until the present. I was there when your mother bore you, and when you bore your children, and I will accept your praise as long as you live. Rest assured that I am watching your children's growth and am eager to begin walking with them.

FROM PSALM 71:5–7

WARRANTY NOTES: THE PSALMIST DECLARES THAT HIS CONFIDENCE HAS BEEN IN THE LORD SINCE HIS YOUTH—EVEN SINCE HIS BIRTH. THE WORD TELLS US THAT EVEN SMALL CHILDREN CAN WALK WITH THE LORD.

Dear God, it's wonderful that I can start my children early on the path to You. Show me ways I can reveal and exalt You before them. Amen.

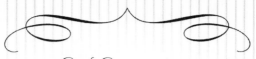

God Guarantees

I WILL INSTRUCT
YOUR CHILDREN

Since your youth, I have shown you My ways. And since your youth, you have praised Me. The same is available to your children: wisdom, insight, knowledge, and godliness. I promise to answer every child's prayer and to fill every child's request for knowledge of My way of life. I am ready to teach as soon as they are ready to learn!

FROM PSALM 71:17

WARRANTY NOTES: GOD'S INSTRUCTION IS AVAILABLE TO ANYONE WHO WANTS IT: WISE OR WEAK, RICH OR FLOUNDERING, OLD OR YOUNG. EVEN CHILDREN CAN SIT AT HIS FEET AND DISCOVER HIS PATH TO LIFE.

Dear God, in many ways I am only a child.
Please continue to teach me Your ways that I
may applaud Your marvelous deeds. And please
continue to reveal Yourself to my children as well.
Amen.

God Guarantees

I HAVE GIVEN YOUR CHILDREN A VAST INHERITANCE

Through you, I have passed along to your children the greatest gift one can give another: the ability to live a life of love, joy, peace, and purpose. My blessings pass from generation to generation—as long as the parents faithfully remember My ways. You can be assured that your children's ability to attain an abundant life is as certain as yours.

FROM DEUTERONOMY 29:29

WARRANTY NOTES: THIS GIFT CAN'T BE CONTAINED OR LIMITED—EXCEPT BY YOUR EXAMPLE.

Dear God, show my children, through me, the way to the best life possible—one lived in Your grace. Surround them with godly friends and influences that can also help them find their way, as we all work for their good.
Amen.

God Guarantees

YOUR CHILD'S ENEMIES ARE MY ENEMIES

When you bless children, you bless Me. They are so valuable to Me that you can be sure their enemies will receive unspeakable punishments. Children are jewels in My eyes. Anyone who makes a child sin or lose his faith in Me is doomed; he would be better off drowning himself than facing My anger.

FROM MATTHEW 18:5–6

WARRANTY NOTES: GOD WANTS OUR CHILDREN TO LIVE LIVES OF FAITH. THOSE WHO LEAD CHILDREN ASTRAY FROM SUCH FAITH DAMAGE THE SOUL. GOD TAKES AWFUL ACTION AGAINST THE ENEMIES OF CHILDREN.

Dear God, thank You for loving my children even more than I do. I can't protect their faith, but You can. I can't face down their foes, but You can. Thank You for Your covering love for those I love most.

Amen.

Four

God's Guarantees about Your Prayers

God Guarantees

I LOVE TO HEAR
FROM YOU

"Pray continually" (NIV)—this is My way of telling you that I want to hear from you often, daily, constantly! I know how many issues concern you, especially those involving your children. Bring those worries to Me—I promise to hear and heed them. My door is never closed.

FROM 1 THESSALONIANS 5:17

WARRANTY NOTES: IT'S EASY TO FALL INTO THE TRAP OF TALKING ABOUT GOD MORE THAN WE TALK TO HIM. MAKE IT A HABIT TO ADDRESS YOUR THOUGHTS TO HIM.

Dear God,
Thank You for this lifeline of prayer.
Forgive me for ignoring it so often.
Please hear me today as I offer You my bundle of
concerns and ask Your wisdom in coping with each one.
Amen.

God Guarantees

PRAYER IS A
BETTER WAY

I don't want you to be anxious or distressed about *anything*. I want to weave your prayers for help into songs of deliverance. I promise to do this when you are ready to make the exchange: peace for petitions, calming down for calling out. Show your children the way I faithfully answer by presenting your requests to Me—often.

FROM PHILIPPIANS 4:6

WARRANTY NOTES: OFTEN WE TRY EVERY-THING BEFORE WE TRY PRAYER. THIS IS A TENDENCY WORTH SHAKING!

Dear God,
Some days I feel free as a bird; others, as burdened as Atlas. How quickly I forget that You are ready to turn my painful fears into signs of Your faithfulness.
Thank You for this gift.
Amen.

God Guarantees

YOUR GOD IS CLOSE BY

Is your child's problem making your soul ragged? Do you lack answers? Do you feel alone in your struggle to help him? I am near you, close to you—always right here when you call to Me. Can you think of any other religion that boasts a God so great and so near to His people when they pray?

FROM DEUTERONOMY 4:7

WARRANTY NOTES: PRAYER IS THE BEST COMMUNICATION DEVICE AVAILABLE—IT CONNECTS THE ALL-TOO-HUMAN WITH THE SUBLIMELY SUPERNATURAL!

Dear God,
My child is suffering today, and I with him.
Here we are, riding on the wings of prayer,
recognizing You and asking for Your help.
Help us know the peace of Your closeness.
Amen.

God Guarantees

TIME DEVOTED TO ME
IS TIME WELL SPENT

My Son knew that without moments spent quietly with Me, the crowds' demands would diminish His strength. The same is true for you: As you care for your children's many needs and requests, yours get lost. You forget to pray, and renewal lingers just outside your grasp. Withdraw from turmoil and spend a few minutes in a lonely place, like My Son did. There, offer Me the activities that threaten to overtake you; I promise to meet you whenever you'd like.

FROM LUKE 5:16

WARRANTY NOTES: TIME WITH GOD MAKES ANY DAY DOABLE.

Dear God, go with me today through my myriad appointments and tasks. Let my children see through me that You are the glue that holds all of life together.
Amen.

God Guarantees

ASKING FOR PRAYER
OPENS MY DOOR

Paul, who prayed for the salvation of the Gentiles and for the sanctification of the saved, asked for prayer, knowing well the essential energies of prayer. I showed him that asking other believers for their strength through prayer is what opens doors for My message. I promise that as you reach out and ask others to join with you on behalf of your children's salvation and sanctification—which really encompass all of their lives—I will reach back.

FROM COLOSSIANS 4:2–3

WARRANTY NOTES: IT'S NOT CLEAR WHO NEEDS PRAYER MORE: THE PRAYED-FOR OR THE PRAY-ER.

Dear God, today I am doing it: I am asking for prayer for my children and for myself as their mother. I ask for all You have for us—wisdom, love, faithfulness—as we seek to serve You as a family. Amen.

God Guarantees

Praying for Your Enemies Will Change You

As you bring the problematic people in your life and your children's lives to Me for help, you will experience knowing Me as Father in an even greater way. Don't be surprised if the one helped is you. You can be certain that as you lift up your enemies, elements of forgiveness will erupt inside you. It's very hard to hate someone you're praying for.

FROM MATTHEW 5:44–45

WARRANTY NOTES: WHAT A RELIEF! GOD DOES MORE THAN ATTEND TO THOSE WE PRAY FOR—HE TOUCHES THOSE OF US WHO PRAY!

Dear God, people and situations in our family members' lives threaten our peace and attack our contentment. Please encourage them today and bring them joy. And would You do the same for us?

Amen.

God Guarantees

YOU CAN CALL
ME DADDY

It was true for Jesus because He was My Son; it is true for you because you are My daughter. As your children address you with affection in their voices, saying, "Mommy," "Mama," or "Mom," so you can come to Me with the same assurance and confidence. You can count on Me to respond with boundless love, so please, call Me "Abba, Daddy."

FROM ROMANS 8:15

WARRANTY NOTES: IT'S FOR KEEPS—FAMILIES ARE FOREVER.

Dear God,
Thank You for loving me as
only a perfect Father can.
I love You in return as only
a well-loved child can.
Amen.

God Guarantees

YOUR PRAYER PREPARES YOUR CHILD'S FUTURE

"I prayed for this child.... So now I give him to the LORD" (NIV). Samuel's mother was a brave and wise woman. Can you follow her example in spirit? I guarantee that your child, devoted to My care through your prayers, is one whose future is full of hope and companionship—Mine. Is there any safer place?

FROM 1 SAMUEL 1:27–28

WARRANTY NOTES: GOD IS THE ONLY ONE WHO LOVES YOUR CHILD EVEN MORE THAN YOU DO.

Dear God,
I, too, prayed for this child, and You gave him to me.
So today I give him back to his Creator
and ask Your faithful interference in his life.
Help us both to give You glory.
Amen.

God Guarantees

I WILL MEET YOU
WHEREVER YOU ARE

Paul prayed from prison. Jesus prayed from a cross. And Jonah cried out from inside a fish. I don't care where you call from—just call. I promise to hear, just as you hear every whimper from your child, no matter what his need.

FROM JONAH 2:1

WARRANTY NOTES: YOU DON'T NEED A PHONE—OR A PHONE BOOTH. JUST CALL HIM.

Dear God,
Thanks for loving me so much that
You hear my every whisper for help.
I've whispered a lot lately,
and I'm grateful Your ears are keen to my cries.
Amen.

PRAYER GLORIFIES ME

No matter what troubles you or your children, I want you to remember what is waiting for you. Think for a few minutes about a place where love rules, peace is palpable, and contentment knows no limit. Look toward that place where prayer takes you, because it's there that I will give you the glory you need in order to glorify Me.

FROM JOHN 17:1

WARRANTY NOTES: THIS IS ALL TEMPORARY, SO INVEST IN SOMETHING ETERNAL— HEAVEN.

Dear God,
It's so easy to forget the grand
destination before me.
I praise You for this unspeakable
hope of Your glory,
as well as for the anticipation that
builds in me as I pray.
Amen.

Five

God's

Guarantees

about Your

Wisdom

God Guarantees

I HAVE ESTABLISHED YOU AS A TEACHER FOR YOUR CHILDREN

You can be certain that as a mother, you are your child's primary source for learning right from wrong, how to make joyous rather than sorrowful choices. What you teach—through your words, actions, and attitudes—lays a foundation for wisdom in your child's life. Your teaching serves as a light that shows the path to righteousness.

FROM PROVERBS 6:20, 23

WARRANTY NOTES: MODELING WISDOM IS SOMETHING MOTHERS DO ALL THE TIME— OR NOT.

Dear God, I long to be a mother whose teaching is consistent, whose words reflect Your Word. Please guide me down the way of righteousness that I may also lead my children there. Amen.

God Guarantees

My Wisdom Is Yours for the Asking

If ever you need guidance or a clear mind in your parenting, just ask for it. I don't blame you for not knowing everything. I am a generous God—eager to pour out all the wisdom you long for. I have storehouses full, and I'm ready to share!

FROM JAMES 1:5

WARRANTY NOTES: A WISE WOMAN KNOWS WHEN TO ASK FOR HELP.

Dear God,
I am not sure what to do about a conflict today.
I have so many options and ideas—
which is the best one?
Thank You for making wisdom so available to me,
and please show me what choice is wisest.
Amen.

God Guarantees

I WILL SHOW YOU
THE WAY TO GO

I promise that you and your children are never alone—even when it feels like you are! You can always rest assured that I will instruct you, guide you, advise you, and watch over you and your family. I am a faithful counselor to all who seek sure guidance.

FROM PSALM 32:8

WARRANTY NOTES: GOD IS AS EAGER TO LEAD AS WE ARE TO FOLLOW!

Dear God,
So many times I don't know which way to go.
Remind me to look to You at each crossroads
and observe each road sign and turn—even when
I don't know where the path is taking me.
I will ever listen to Your counsel as you
faithfully watch over us.
Amen.

I HAVE SENT A HELPER

I am not just above you in the heavens; I am with you on the earth. I have sent My Spirit to show you truth. He will speak only the words I give Him. Know that He will guide you.

FROM JOHN 16:13

WARRANTY NOTES: HOW COMFORTING TO KNOW WE HAVE A GUIDE WHO IS NEARER TO US THAN EVEN AIR. HE IS WITHIN—REVEALING, COMFORTING, AND REMINDING US THAT WE ARE GOD'S.

Dear God,
I am so grateful to know that You have provided
a constant companion in this journey of life.
As a mom, I need lots of wisdom—and reassurance.
Help me to hear the voice of Your Spirit
as I make each choice.
Amen.

God Guarantees

I HAVE PREPARED AMAZING THINGS FOR YOU

No one person knows—or can even imagine—the amazing things I have prepared for those who love Me. Expect good to come your way; watch for it! Know that it is from Me, that I designed it with love and will reveal it to you.

FROM 1 CORINTHIANS 2:9–10

WARRANTY NOTES: GOD'S PLAN FOR YOU AND YOUR FAMILY IS A FULL AND SURPRISING ONE—ONE THAT INCLUDES JOY.

Dear God,
Sometimes I try to plan my own way, or the ways of my children. How foolish my arrangements sometimes turn out to be. Please help me to walk in Your plan instead and to remember to thank You for every good thing You send to those who love You.
Amen.

God Guarantees

WALKING IN WISDOM BRINGS YOU SAFETY

You can do no greater thing than seek wisdom and live by what you learn. Though you may have to sacrifice something and even make an effort to hold on to understanding, go after it. You can be sure that understanding will protect you from unseen and unexpected evil, lift you to new heights, and bring you honor.

FROM PROVERBS 4:6–8

WARRANTY NOTES: IF YOU LONG FOR THE COMFORT OF A HIDING PLACE FROM THE WORLD'S TROUBLES, YOU HAVE IT—IN GOD'S PERFECT AND RICH WISDOM, LAID OUT FOR YOU IN HIS WORD.

Dear God, surely I need wisdom today, and every day.
I want to be safe from the influence of evil and show
my children how to walk in the shelter of Your Word.
Thank You for offering us this source of protection.
Amen.

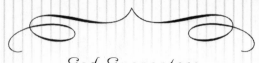

REVERENCE FOR ME OPENS THE DOOR TO WISDOM

The woman who fears Me—who honors Me with her mind, heart, soul, and strength—is the one I will guide. You will know what choice to make, which path to choose, which way is best for you. I will instruct you.

FROM PSALM 25:12

WARRANTY NOTES: IT'S THAT SIMPLE. THOSE WHO HONOR GOD WILL KNOW HIS WISDOM.

Dear God,
How frequently I forget to fear You
and to show that I know You are God.
Please forgive me for losing sight of Your power
and love. I worship You today with all my life
and being and offer myself for Your leading.
Amen.

God Guarantees

YOU WILL NOT
STUMBLE IN THE DARK

I know every obstacle hidden in darkness, every foe set against you. I am full of light, and when you find yourself in dark places, I will illuminate the way out. You are never at the mercy of unseen enemies, for My light reveals and overwhelms them. As you follow Me, your life will be lit even in the midst of this world's darkness.

FROM JOHN 8:12

WARRANTY NOTES: NIGHTTIME ARRIVES REGULARLY—HAVE YOU NOTICED? LET THE BRIGHTNESS OF THE LORD GUIDE AND SUSTAIN YOU IN ALL CIRCUMSTANCES.

Dear God, everyone is afraid of the dark sometimes. When I feel threatened or anxious or attacked, darkness seems to fall around me. I cry out to You to lead me from the dark places with the light of Your love. Thank You for being a constant "flashlight" in my life.

Amen.

I OFFER YOU A LIFE OF MEANING AND ENJOYMENT

To the mom who pleases Me, I promise to impart life's best gifts: wisdom to know her way, the comfort of My knowledge, and rich satisfaction in each of her tasks.

FROM ECCLESIASTES 2:26

WARRANTY NOTES: WHAT MORE COULD A PERSON WANT? TO PLEASE GOD IS CLEARLY A WIN-WIN SITUATION. HE GETS GLORY, AND WE GET EVERYTHING WE NEED FOR LASTING HAPPINESS AND WISE LIVING!

Dear God, serving You is the only way to go. I am so grateful for the exchange—my obedience for Your gifts. I desire to please You. Thank You for generously providing all I need to honor You in my life. Help me to teach my children how to honor You as well. Amen.

I WILL MAKE YOUR PATHS CLEAR

As you exercise your trust in Me—letting go of what you know and asking for My wisdom—your way will become obvious. Remembering that I alone see all, know all, and sustain all will encourage you to give Me your whole heart's faith. I guarantee that I will reward your devotion with guidance.

FROM PROVERBS 3:5–6

WARRANTY NOTES: THE WAY TO WISDOM IS CLEAR—IT IS THROUGH GOD. ONCE WE ACKNOWLEDGE HIS SOVEREIGNTY AND LET GO OF OUR OWN UNDERSTANDING, WE POSITION OURSELVES TO RECEIVE HIS GUIDANCE.

Dear God, thank You for asking such a simple thing of me—trust. I trust You today to show me how to handle the struggles I face and the questions my children ask. My own knowledge is too limited for this calling of motherhood, and I lean on You.

Amen.

Six

God's
Guarantees
about His
Faithfulness

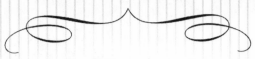

God Guarantees

I WILL BE WITH YOUR CHILD WHEREVER HE GOES

Because I love your child, he need never be terrified or discouraged. Teach him to be strong and courageous because I am behind, before, and alongside him in every endeavor—he can count on Me.

FROM JOSHUA 1:9

WARRANTY NOTES: GOD HAS PROMISED ELSEWHERE IN SCRIPTURE THAT ANGELS WATCH OVER OUR CHILDREN. HERE HE REMINDS US THAT HE HIMSELF IS JUST AS CLOSE! THAT SHOULD COMFORT BOTH US AND OUR CHILDREN.

Dear God,
Thank You for walking beside me and my child. What a relief to know that You love him enough to accompany him through life. Thanks for being close to him today.
Amen.

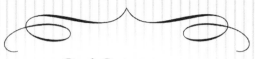

God Guarantees

I WILL NEVER
FORSAKE YOUR CHILD

You need to know how devoted I am to the child who follows Me: I will never, ever leave him. Even if you or your husband were to forsake him, I won't! I am God and My faithfulness is solid, complete, limitless. Rest assured that I consider your child *My child.*

FROM PSALM 27:10

WARRANTY NOTES: AS COMMITTED AS YOU ARE TO YOUR CHILD—BONE-DEEP, OR DEEPER—GOD IS EVEN MORE PASSIONATE ABOUT HIS CARE.

Dear God,
I'm so glad my child isn't dependent on
my faithfulness, because I fail. You don't,
and I will teach him this in every way I can.
Amen.

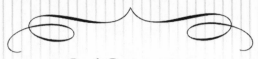

God Guarantees

YOUR CHILD'S INHERITANCE IS SET FOR LIFE

My people are always that—My people. Therefore your child, once he becomes Mine as well, will enjoy an everlasting heritage. My Word declares that those who are Mine stay Mine. Rest assured that your child will know My care eternally, that he enjoys the certainty of heaven and its rewards.

FROM PSALM 94:14

WARRANTY NOTES: NO EARTHLY INHERITANCE CAN COMPARE. HERE WILLS AND DESTINIES CAN BE CHANGED. THE ONES WRITTEN BY GOD CANNOT. HE BROOKS NO INTERFERENCE WHEN IT COMES TO HIS CHILDREN'S FUTURE.

Dear God, what a rich thought: When they follow You, my children are set for life. This thought comforts me as Your child today. Thank You.

Amen.

God Guarantees

I Control Your Child's Circumstances

I not only made your child; I designed every circumstance around him—his parents, his siblings, his friends and relatives, his home, his school, his opportunities. The earth is mine, and I shape it for its inhabitants' good. Believe that your child has every benefit he needs to succeed and to glorify Me and that I will not call him to do anything I have not equipped him to do.

FROM PSALM 24:1

WARRANTY NOTES: IT'S A MASTERFUL PLAN—NO CALLING WITHOUT EQUIPPING!

Dear God, sometimes I feel unsure that I can give my child everything he needs in life—but You can and You have. I feel calm knowing that You take care of the details beyond my arranging—that Your holy interference can be counted on for good in my child's life.
Amen.

God Guarantees

I WILL REWARD YOUR CHILD'S OBEDIENCE

The child who follows Me—who refuses to cheat at school or abuse a friendship, who honors his parents and tells the truth—is the one I select for blessing. I will be his defender, vindicator, and friend.

FROM PSALM 24:4–5

WARRANTY NOTES: A GOOD KID IS HARD TO FIND—BUT EASY TO BLESS!

Dear God,
Thanks for promising to notice every
effort my child makes.
Thank You for celebrating even
their attempts to obey.
I celebrate them with You today.
Amen.

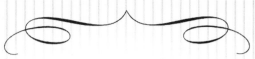

God Guarantees

I WILL REMIND YOUR CHILD OF ALL YOU HAVE TAUGHT HIM

The training you give your child is something I coat with permanence. When you teach him My ways, you can be certain that in the end he will not depart from them. I will remind him of holy choices throughout his life. He will always have this knowledge as a guide.

FROM PROVERBS 22:6

WARRANTY NOTES: THERE IS NO EXPIRATION DATE ON GOD'S WISDOM—OR HIS FAITHFULNESS TO YOUR CHILD.

Dear God, thank You for making sure that my words—and Your Word—are not wasted. I so long for them to bear fruit in my child's life, but I'm not always in a position to offer them at the right times. You are. Please do this, that my child may give You glory.
Amen.

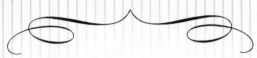

God Guarantees

My Promises Are for Your Children

Children are as good at receiving gifts as their parents are—maybe even better! This is why I designed My plan of salvation in both kid and adult sizes. My promise is to you *and* your children—those near and those far-off. If any child invites Me in, I will come and fill his life with My presence.

FROM ACTS 2:39

WARRANTY NOTES: EVEN CHILDREN HAVE ROOM INSIDE FOR GOD.

Dear God,
Thank You for inviting my child to
take part in Your gift of salvation.
I know no greater gift.
Thank You for offering it to me as well.
Amen.

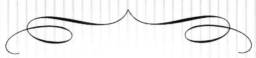

I PLANT DREAMS IN YOUR CHILD

I made a promise long ago, and I have begun to fulfill it: I am pouring out My Spirit on the young and the old. Know that through the Spirit your children will have visions and dreams and imagine wonderful outcomes—and they will pursue them, with My power. Just as you hope your children will be blessings in the world, so do I—and I have designed ways for them to do that! I will be faithful to help them along the way.

FROM ACTS 2:17

WARRANTY NOTES: DREAMS START US ON AMAZING, GOD-FILLED JOURNEYS.

*Dear God, please plant a dream in my child—
a way of serving You that perhaps no one has thought
of before. I will do all I can to "grow" this seed and
with You watch its fulfillment.*

Amen.

God Guarantees

I WILL ENTRUST YOUR CHILD WITH RESPONSIBILITY

As your child proves his faithfulness to Me, I will prove My faithfulness to him. When he shows that My trust in him—to refute peer pressure and make wise choices, to stand with the weak against the bully, to tell the truth when a lie would do— was a good investment, I will entrust him with more. And the rewards will match his response!

FROM MATTHEW 25:21

WARRANTY NOTES: GOD WILL NEVER SHORT-CHANGE YOUR CHILD—OR YOU. FAITHFULNESS IS HIS DELIGHT!

Dear God,
I pray that my child would grow stronger from each successful encounter with temptation, that he may prove worthy of Your investment. I pray the same for me.
Amen.

God Guarantees

YOUR CHILD WILL HAVE
REASON TO PRAISE ME

A person with a humble heart sees all the ways I have blessed, upheld, delivered, advised, corrected, and equipped him. So it will be with your child as he lives a reverent life before Me. Teach him to serve Me with all his heart and to always remember all I've done for him. Know that as he serves wisely he will have reason to praise Me for all I do on his behalf.

FROM 1 SAMUEL 12:24

WARRANTY NOTES: FEW TRUE WIN-WIN SITUATIONS EXIST IN THIS WORLD, BUT SERVING GOD IS ONE OF THEM.

Dear God,
I praise You today for all You have done and all
You will do for my child as he embraces Your ways.
Make us aware of all the ways You bless us so
that we may honor You.
Amen.

Seven

God's
Guarantees
about Your
Peace of Mind

God Guarantees

RIGHT LIVING
BRINGS PEACE

Despite the turmoil around you—terrorism, financial recession, your own family's worries—you can experience the longed-for results of righteous living: peace, quietness, confidence, a secure home, and undisturbed rest. I guarantee that those who live a Spirit-filled life will enjoy a blessing-rich life.

FROM ISAIAH 32:17–18

WARRANTY NOTES: LIVING IN STEP WITH GOD'S SPIRIT BRINGS NOTHING BUT THE BEST RESULT POSSIBLE: PEACE OF MIND.

Dear God,
The struggles in the world around me are one thing—
the fears we deal with in our family are another. They
seem far more important and frightening. Thank You for
the inviting offer of peace. I'll take it!
Amen.

MY PEACE IS THE GREATEST KIND

What troubles your children, and therefore troubles you, today? Nightmares? Illness? A school bully, or sibling power struggles? No matter their size, these pains are very real—but so is the peace I bring you. I don't give as the world gives—reluctantly or inconsistently—but freely and continually. Rest assured that I am with you, and with your children, in the turmoil life brings. Don't be afraid. Be at peace.

FROM JOHN 14:27

WARRANTY NOTES: THEY'RE THE THREE MOST WELCOME WORDS IN THE BIBLE: DON'T BE AFRAID.

Dear God, I come today with the worries of my children. Please give us wisdom in dealing with these, but above all, please give us Your peace. From that will flow perspective, creativity, and rest.

Amen.

God Guarantees

I Have Equipped You for Peaceful and Powerful Living

In your work to be a wise mother and strong example to your children, I have sent you a powerful equipper: the Holy Spirit. I guarantee that He is a wellspring of power and strength and can give you a sound mind. Never forget that you have this companion who walks with you through every difficulty, who offers help in every calamity.

FROM 2 TIMOTHY 1:7

Warranty Notes: A strong spirit can overcome weak flesh any day.

Dear God,
Thank You for giving me a companion.
I surely need His supernatural insight today.
I pray that, as a mom and as Your disciple,
I will bring You glory.
Amen.

God Guarantees

I WILL ESTABLISH
YOUR PEACE

Are concerns ricocheting through your mind? Is focus distant? Do you lack perspective or insight—peace? Turn your mind toward Me. I will keep you in perfect peace as your mind stays on Me. I promise that as you practice trust, it will become a habit. Your mind will settle, clarity will come, and you will enjoy rest.

FROM ISAIAH 26:3

WARRANTY NOTES: A CLUTTERED MIND IS A WORRIED MIND. DO SOME CLEANING.

Dear God,
Please help me to focus my thoughts—
and hope—on You today.
I trust You to intervene in all these situations,
and I commit myself to Your care. It's a habit I want to
develop. Thank You for the promise of peace.
Amen.

God Guarantees

I AM YOUR GOD

I know you feel small amid your troubles today. The fact is that you *are* small—but I am not. Don't be dismayed, but remember that I am God. Just as you surround your young child with love and devotion, so I as your Father envelop you today. I promise I will uphold you with My righteous right hand.

FROM ISAIAH 41:10

WARRANTY NOTES: IT'S GOOD TO KNOW THAT OUR SMALLNESS IS LESS A FLAW THAN AN OPPORTUNITY FOR GOD'S "BIGNESS" TO SHINE.

Dear God,
I want to lose myself in Your greatness today.
You are the Lord; You are my God.
Therefore, all about me will be well.
Praise You for this assurance.
Amen.

God Guarantees

I CALL YOU TO A CHEERFUL LIFE

My Son warned His disciples—and you—that they would have trouble in this world, and you know how right He was. Conflicts within the family and without, worldly dangers, and fears close to home—an insecure or sad child—all threaten any sense of well-being you try to have. I know. I sent Jesus for this purpose—that you might have peace despite all. I promise that you can be cheerful in the midst of struggle because I have overcome the world and all its harms. I did it for you.

FROM JOHN 16:33

WARRANTY NOTES: WHAT A GREAT INVITA-TION—BE CHEERFUL! IT SURE BEATS GLOOM.

Dear God, I embrace your Son today. I lift up the one(s) in our family who especially need(s) comfort this day. Make us a family of cheerful hearts that trust in You.

Amen.

God Guarantees

I Will Show You a Way through Tough Times

I know that temptation is rife around you: temptation to give in to fear, to take the easy way out, to try to rescue your children rather than let them learn to make wise choices. You can rest assured that no temptation comes to you without a way of escape as well. Watch for these! Teach your children how to spot them. I promise that I will allow no temptation to overwhelm you.

FROM 1 CORINTHIANS 10:13

WARRANTY NOTES: WHAT A RELIEF TO KNOW THAT TEMPTATION ALWAYS TRAVELS WITH A TWIN: ESCAPE.

Dear God, thanks for recognizing our weakness and offering a means of rescue. Today I promise to look for every way out of temptation. I do want to give You glory.
Amen.

CONTENTMENT IS YOURS

Contentment sometimes seems elusive, I know. But it is actually always within reach. Look today at all you have and add up even the "small" things, such as food and clothing. Simple gratitude (contentment) plus godly behavior equals unspeakable riches. Know that I offer such wealth to you.

FROM 1 TIMOTHY 6:6

WARRANTY NOTES: ARE YOU RICH TODAY AND YOU JUST DIDN'T KNOW IT?

Dear God,
I am grateful for all You have provided
for me and my family.
I long to bless You with my contentment
and a respectful response of gratitude.
Will You accept my offering of thanks today?
Amen.

God Guarantees

I WILL GIVE YOU MORE

The American way—more, more, more—isn't My way. The "more" that I want to give you involves holy intangibles: love, satisfaction, peace of mind. Let your heart be without covetousness and be content instead. Seek these things through me. I promise that they will be "more" than enough.

FROM HEBREWS 13:5

WARRANTY NOTES: PEACE COMES FROM A FULL HEART, NOT A FULL PURSE.

Dear God,
Forgive me for empty wishes.
Possessions and cash are so appealing—
they seem to offer so much satisfaction.
Fill my heart with You instead.
That will be riches enough for me.
Amen.

God Guarantees

YOU WILL NOT
BE OVERCOME

Because I love you, I will not allow you to be consumed by your troubles. My compassion will fall on you freshly every morning, and I will show you faithful love. Wait for My deliverance; watch for My rescue. I never fail, so you have constant hope.

FROM LAMENTATIONS 3:22–25

WARRANTY NOTES: THERE IS NO MORE PERFECT GUARANTEE THAN THAT GOD WILL SAVE US.

Dear God,
Thanks for Your presence, Your assurance,
and Your power.
I submit myself and my
family to Your care today,
and I watch for Your deliverance.
Amen.

Eight

God's

Guarantees

about Your

State of Grace

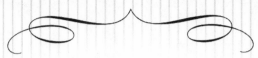

God Guarantees

I FORGET YOUR MISTAKES

Mistakes are bad enough in themselves; the guilt that follows can cripple. When you, in a weak moment, raise your voice to your child, use harsh words, or fail to discipline, you sense your failure immediately. As soon as you confess, I promise to wipe the slate clean. You are free to start fresh. The blood of My Son is a powerful cleanser when sin tries to stain.

FROM 1 JOHN 1:9

WARRANTY NOTES: IT'S A CURIOUS TRUTH: NO ONE IS MORE EAGER TO FORGIVE THAN THE ONE WE OFFEND MOST—OUR HEAVENLY FATHER.

Dear God, I blew it today more times than I can count. Please forgive me and draw me close to Yourself. Thanks for being such a patient Father. Make me a patient mother so I can forgive my children as You forgive me.

Amen.

God Guarantees

I HAVE MADE PEACE WITH YOU ALWAYS

It is My pleasure to save you! I was pleased to send My Son on your behalf to provide a way of salvation. The mission was so successful that peace is now possible between Me and *anyone*. I'm so glad you have taken advantage of this grace—now you and I enjoy an eternal, tranquil, and life-giving relationship. This was My goal all along, and it is My guarantee today.

FROM COLOSSIANS 1:19–20

WARRANTY NOTES: THINK ABOUT WHAT PEACE MEANS—A TOTAL LACK OF UNREST, DISTRUST, AND TURMOIL.

Dear God, I must disappoint You so often. It's hard for me to understand how You could pursue me to be Yours. Yet grace is something I immerse myself in, and I know that brings You glory, however many mistakes I make.

Amen.

God Guarantees

MY GRACE IS BOUNDLESS

The nature of My grace—its immeasurable height and depth, breadth and width—is a bountiful stream that runs constantly, bathes gently, and succors all who thirst for it. This is the grace I call you to and promise you. You and your family will receive one blessing after another. Grace's benefits will never be numbered.

FROM JOHN 1:16

WARRANTY NOTES: GRACE IS A GIFT THAT KEEPS GIVING, NO MATTER HOW MUCH WE USE IT.

Dear God,
Thanks for providing not only forgiveness,
but also grace that inspires me to keep working
at this role of mother. If You didn't give me Your grace,
I wouldn't know how to continue.
Thanks for this eternal gift.
Amen.

God Guarantees

MY GRACE WILL ENCOURAGE YOU AND YOUR CHILDREN

When you see your children taking baby steps toward Me—choosing kindness over harshness or sharing instead of hoarding—cheer them on. Grace is beginning its work in their lives. Encourage them, by word and example, to remain true to the God they are starting to serve. I guarantee I will honor your efforts—and those of your children.

FROM ACTS 11:23

WARRANTY NOTES: EVEN CHILDREN NEED GRACE—FOR BOTH RECEIVING FORGIVENESS AND OFFERING IT.

Dear God, I already see so much evidence of Your grace in my children's lives. Lord, please continue to train my children through me to practice grace in all their dealings. And help me to do the same.
Amen.

GRACE MAKES YOU WHO YOU ARE SUPPOSED TO BE

Paul is a shining example of what My grace does. Once a hater and persecutor, he became proclaimer, teacher, and friend. My work in his life shows! Know that My grace will also be revealed in you, as you rest in its soft folds of forgiveness. You are what you are meant to be: a mom, fully forgiven and free to obey Me!

FROM 1 CORINTHIANS 15:10

WARRANTY NOTES: GRACE IS NOT ONLY EFFECTIVE—IT IS PERMANENT!

Dear God,
In my failures I have tried to plumb the depths of
Your grace—much like Paul did—and I can joyfully
report that it has no end. I praise You for this.
Amen.

God Guarantees

GRACE IS
EMPOWERING

Today I bless you and keep you; My face is shining upon you. I pour My grace on you. I am watching over you and sending you peace. Why? Because when you receive My grace, you are certain to extend it in gentle words, warm hugs, and kind words for your child. Love begets love—I promise.

FROM NUMBERS 6:24–26

WARRANTY NOTES: PSSST—PASS IT ON!

Dear God,
I accept Your gift today,
and I promise to share it with
everyone in my family.
This is so they will be blessed—
and You will too.
Amen.

God Guarantees

GRACE GOES TO
THE HUMBLE

I've designed a special garment for you, one that you must wear daily. I promise that something wonderful will result! The coat is humility, and the benefit it always delivers is access to My grace—something everyone needs but few are willing to ask for. The proud, you see, deny their need for it, and their arrogance is offensive. Humble folk like you attract my attention and my blessing. I long to envelop you in saving, inspiring grace. So just try it on....

FROM 1 PETER 5:5

WARRANTY NOTES: ONE SIZE FITS ALL—ALL THE HUMBLE, THAT IS.

Dear God,
I will gladly wear Your coat of grace. As a woman
and a mother, I freely admit my need for such
a garment and praise You for creating it!
Amen.

God Guarantees

MY GRACIOUS HAND IS ON YOU

It was said of My servant Ezra that "the gracious hand of his God was on him" (NIV). I want you to know that it is also upon you and all those who accept My Son and follow My Word. This means that My favor rests on you, My ears are open to your cries, and My eyes are upon every good example you give your children. As you journey through your life with Me, I guarantee that My power is holding you up, and My Son is interceding for your success. Blessing is yours—enjoy it!

FROM EZRA 7:9

WARRANTY NOTES: GRACE IS NOT JUST FOR MOMS BUT FOR KIDS TOO—REMIND THEM OF IT TODAY.

Dear God, I sense Your goodness surrounding and filling me today, Lord. I don't understand it but I accept it—and offer it back to You in service.
Amen.

YOU ARE ENRICHED
IN EVERY WAY

You bear the fruit of My Spirit. You are clearly equipped to minister on My behalf as you wait for My Son to return. I see this in the way you answer your child's demands with quiet words, or take a deep breath before tangling with another's prickly personality. I will keep you strong to the end and stand you spotless before Me on Jesus' day. I have called you into fellowship with My Son; I am faithful; and I will fulfill every promise I have made.

FROM 1 CORINTHIANS 1:4–9

WARRANTY NOTES: GRACE MEANS OUR REPORT CARDS READ A+ DESPITE THE FACT THAT WE SOMETIMES FLUNK THE POP QUIZ.

Dear God, thank You for reminding me of all the things I do right. Mistakes loom largest in my vision, and I need Your encouragement. Praise You for grace that fills in for my failures—what a comfort to a mom! Amen.

God Guarantees

GRACE MAKES
YOU CONFIDENT

Let grace erase your fear. Your right standing with Me, because of Jesus' blood, means you and I are friends. When you have a need, approach My throne with all the confidence of someone who expects a swift and helpful answer—for that is what I will give you. My mercy flows freely, and your share is always ready.

FROM HEBREWS 4:16

WARRANTY NOTES: GRACE REPLACES FEAR WITH CONFIDENCE—IF YOU LET IT.

Dear God,
You are dear and You are my God—I accept Your grace.
I come before Your throne, holding my children's hands,
confident that You will hear and respond and that
mercy makes a way for us. I praise You.
Amen.

Nine

God's
Guarantees
about Your
Child's Potential

God Guarantees

YOURS IS A CHILD OF PROMISE

As your child embraces and seeks Me, I promise that I will fill him with My Spirit, My love, and My strength. He will be pleasing in My sight and fruitful in every good work. Know that as your child pursues Me, he will grow in knowledge and have a walk worthy of My name. And he will delight you as well as Me!

FROM COLOSSIANS 1:10

WARRANTY NOTES: EVERY PERSON HAS A DESTINY RICH WITH MEANING AND HOPE— YOUR CHILD IS JUST SUCH A PERSON.

Dear God,
You know that I long for my child to have a saving
and substantial relationship with You. Help me to work
with You as you draw him to Yourself. I believe that
Your hand is on my child.
Amen.

God Guarantees

I WILL HELP YOUR CHILD ACCOMPLISH WONDERFUL THINGS

Your child is very dear to Me. I created him, you birthed him, and now together we will help him walk in the good works I have planned for him from eternity past. Know that I will empower him to do all the amazing things I have planned for him, and I will follow his progress as closely as— even closer than—you do!

FROM EPHESIANS 2:10

WARRANTY NOTES: GOD IS THE POWER BEHIND EVERY GOOD DEED YOUR CHILD ACCOMPLISHES.

Dear God, thank You for Your sweet companionship as I watch and help my child grow. I share Your desire to see him take on mighty tasks and fulfill each one with Your help. Let me teach him by example to call on You always.

Amen.

God Guarantees

I WILL USE YOUR CHILD IN MY SERVICE

Your child may be young, but he is already full of potential. Rest assured that I am already preparing him for a godly life because you have given him to Me. As he chooses to listen for My voice, I will speak to him, advise his every step, and catch him when he stumbles. He is safe in My hands and precious in My sight.

FROM 1 SAMUEL 3:1, 10

WARRANTY NOTES: A CHILD'S PROMISE STARTS AT CONCEPTION.

Dear God,
Thank You for enveloping my child in Your love,
even before he knows You. Thank You for expecting
and planning good things for him—
especially Your presence. Please keep him as the
apple of Your eye, and use him to give You glory.
Amen.

God Guarantees

NONE OF YOUR CHILD'S GODLY ACTIONS WILL FAIL

As I was with young Samuel, so I am with your child. As I called that young boy, gave him opportunity and ability to serve, and ensured his success, so I will with your child. I promise that his wise words will never be wasted; his service will always reap rewards; and his godly desires will always know fulfillment. A child who wants to glorify Me, you see, cannot fail! I won't allow it.

FROM 1 SAMUEL 3:19

WARRANTY NOTES: NO BETTER PROMISE EXISTS: GOD WILL MANAGE YOUR CHILD'S LIFE WITH LOVE AND PROTECTION.

Dear God, I welcome Your management of my child's life. I ask for wisdom to help him on his path, and peace to release him to take risks and face failure.

Amen.

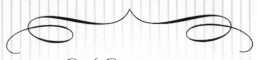

God Guarantees

YOUR CHILDREN HAVE SIGNIFICANT ROLES

Be careful that you don't forget My past faithfulness to you and your family. Remember aloud the things I have done for you, and savor them in your heart. Teach them to your children, as they are purveyors of My truth. Like you, they will pass along life's best lessons to their children. Keep alive your heritage of living by My commands; see that every generation has access to the blessing.

FROM DEUTERONOMY 4:9

WARRANTY NOTES: SEE THAT BY YOUR EXAMPLE GOD'S FAITHFUL WAYS ARE RECORDED IN FAMILY HISTORY.

Dear God, I see that my children are learning from me every day whether Your words are vital or frivolous. Let me give You glory by modeling the wisdom of Your commands, that my children may pass along words of life to those that follow them.

Amen.

God Guarantees

GOD HAS GIFTED YOUR CHILD WITH ABILITIES

To everyone who believes on Me, even your small children, I assign gifts and abilities. Know that even when they are young, your children bear the fingerprints of My endowment. As their mother, don't let such gifts lie dormant, but be a good steward of them for your child. You can be certain that your talents, and those of your children, come directly from My hands, for your pleasure and My service.

FROM 1 PETER 4:10

WARRANTY NOTES: IT'S SAID THAT "IF YOU DON'T USE IT, YOU LOSE IT." MAKE NO MISTAKE: GOD GIVES GIFTS TO BE USED. THE YOUNG ARE NOT EXEMPT FROM PUTTING THEIR TALENTS TO WORK.

Dear God, make my eyes sensitive to the spiritual gifts my children exhibit. Guide me in helping them recognize opportunities to express them. Be glorified in our family.

Amen.

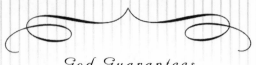

God Guarantees

YOUR INFLUENCE WILL BEAR SWEET FRUIT

You are an essential tool in developing your child's mature and positive character—character that reveals all the potential I created him with. Rest assured that I empower your discipline—what you teach won't be wasted. I promise that the child you raise in My Word and My ways, who seeks to honor Me, will bring you nothing less than delight and peace.

FROM PROVERBS 29:17

WARRANTY NOTES: CHARACTER COMES FROM MANY PLACES, BUT MOM IS ONE OF THE BEST SOURCES.

Dear God, fill me with Your wisdom and energy as I teach my child discipline and good choices. I want to be the best example of sanctified living he has—I want him to want to follow You because of me. I commit my way to You and trust You to fulfill my potential as a godly mom.
Amen.

God Guarantees

I Am Your Child's Keeper

What does your child need today? Protection? Motivation? Encouragement? Healing? Opportunity? I already know the answer, and I promise to supply it. I am your child's keeper—My hand hovers over his head to shade and protect him.

FROM PSALM 121:5–6

WARRANTY NOTES: THE MANUFACTURER IS ALSO THE KEEPER—HE PROMISES LIFE-LONG MAINTENANCE ON HIS EVERY PRODUCT!

Dear God,
Thank You for giving us more than assignments—
You give us the courage and talent to accomplish them.
May my children and I do this today…
and tomorrow.
Amen.

God Guarantees

I MADE YOUR CHILD WONDERFUL

Your child may seem to be just a small seed, but he is the seed of a mighty oak! I created him—specifically and carefully, fearfully and wonderfully. Everything I make is marvelous, and I want you to know this full well. You are the mother of a miracle!

FROM PSALM 139:14–16

WARRANTY NOTES: YOUR CHILD'S LIFE CAN ENRICH THE LIVES OF OTHERS—BUT HE'LL NEED LOTS OF CULTIVATION FIRST!

Dear God,
I am thankful that You want my child to bless others—
I want him to do that too! He is off to a good start,
by blessing me and the rest of our family.
Help him see opportunities to do all the good he can,
and give him the courage to do it.
Amen.

God Guarantees

I WILL PRESERVE YOUR CHILD'S FUTURE

Though he faces trouble, the child who walks with Me will confront it with My power in his hands and heart. Though enemies surround him, he will enjoy the safe parameters of My will. Though his own hands may fail him, Mine won't. I guarantee that I will guard him as I would My own—after all, that is what he is.

FROM PSALM 138:7–8

WARRANTY NOTES: ONE OF GOD'S NAMES IS SAVIOR—FOR GOOD REASON. SAVING IS WHAT HE DOES BEST!

Dear God,
I commit my child's future—and my concerns
about it—to Your saving power and love.
Let us both rest in the certainty of Your salvation,
both now and in eternity.
Amen.

Ten

God's

Guarantees

about His

Sovereignty

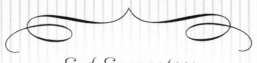

God Guarantees

I AM IN CONTROL OF YOUR CHILD'S DAY

Both day and night are Mine. I created the earth, the sun, and the seasons. If I have done all this, I can and will also establish each day of your life and your child's life. As your child wakes each morning and goes to sleep each night, trust Me. Each and every part of your child's day is under My direction. The light and darkness of life are Mine.

FROM PSALM 74:16–17

WARRANTY NOTES: BECAUSE HE CREATED THE LIGHT AND THE DARK, YOU CAN TRUST HIM EVERY MOMENT OF EVERY DAY.

Dear God,
As the sun rises and sets, I can look to Your creation
and see Your power. I trust in Your incredible creativity.
You will establish and create life and joy and meaning
in my days and my child's days.
Amen.

God Guarantees

ALL THAT I HAVE
IS YOURS AND
YOUR CHILD'S

The picture of the prodigal's father is a picture of My welcome to you and your child always. I will not reject any of My children when they come to Me. And just as I welcomed home the prodigal, I also promised his faithful older brother that all I am and have is his. I give that same promise to you.

FROM LUKE 15:31–32

WARRANTY NOTES: THE OLDER BROTHER WAS ENVIOUS OF HIS PRODIGAL BROTHER'S WARM WELCOME. BUT INSTEAD OF BEING ANGRY OR SCOLDING, HIS FATHER SIMPLY REMINDED HIM OF ALL THE GOOD THINGS HE HAD.

Dear God, thank You for understanding my weaknesses.
As I see You have offered and promised me everything
You have, help me to love and give to my child the same.
Amen.

God Guarantees

I WILL KEEP YOUR CHILD FROM FALLING

I am the One who is able to keep your child from going down and staying down. I will catch you both when you stumble through life's potholes. Grab My hand—and no other—to pull you to your feet. And I am so delighted to tell you that I will ultimately introduce you both before My Father's throne as clean, unblemished children of His.

FROM JUDE 1:24

WARRANTY NOTES: OUR TENDENCY IS TO SLIP; GOD'S TENDENCY IS ALWAYS TO CATCH US.

Dear God, sometimes we flounder and feel like staying down on the ground. Our fears and faults seem bigger than You. But You again pull us up and show us how You see us—clean and spotless. Thank You for always keeping us standing.
Amen.

God Guarantees

I WILL GIVE YOU THE CROWN OF LIFE

I know your life is filled with unpredictable changes and tests. As you love Me and persevere through the challenges and trials of this temporal life, remember that I have promised you a crown. You are blessed because the hard times here on earth will culminate in My promise and the covering of eternal life.

FROM JAMES 1:12

WARRANTY NOTES: WHAT IF THAT HUGE PROBLEM DOES HAVE A HIGHER PURPOSE?

Dear God,
Some days are harder than others as I go through
the tests and trials of parenting and being human
on this earth. I look to You and the promise You
have given us that it will all be worth it in the end.
Thank You for that hope!
Amen.

God Guarantees

I WILL PUT A NEW SPIRIT IN YOUR CHILD

Through Adam and Eve the fall of man brought a spirit of sin, which brings hardness of heart. But I will replace that hardness with a new spirit of softness and vulnerability to Me. When times come that your child seems resistant to Me, I promise to give him an undivided heart of flesh.

FROM EZEKIEL 11:19

WARRANTY NOTES: HE PROMISES A HEART OF FLESH INSTEAD OF STONE. IS THERE ANY QUESTION WHICH WE WOULD CHOOSE?

Dear God,
I see resistance and hardness in my own heart and in my child's. Our sinful nature is real, but Your spirit is more real. I pray for Your softness and openness of heart. I thank You for putting a new spirit—the Holy Spirit —into our hearts.
Amen.

God Guarantees

I WILL MAKE YOUR WORK MEANINGFUL

It is a gift from Me for you to enjoy and find satisfaction in your daily chores and duties. I even grant you enjoyment as you change diapers, make meals, do laundry, and take your kids through all their activities. This is a part of the destiny I have for your life.

FROM ECCLESIASTES 5:18–19

WARRANTY NOTES: GOD HELPS US TO RECOGNIZE THAT THE MOST MUNDANE TASKS IN LIFE HAVE THE POTENTIAL TO BE THE MOST MEANINGFUL.

Dear God,
Today I find contentment and peace as I
perform seemingly meaningless tasks for my child.
Each one matters. Thank You, Lord, for making
me a mom and for bringing me joy and fulfillment
in my day through serving my child.
Amen.

God Guarantees

I Am Accomplishing a New Thing in You

You can forget the past mistakes you've made. Don't let your mind linger on what's done and gone. Where you've seen just wasteland and desert, I am doing something new and fresh. I am forging a trail through what seems like tangled wilderness. Springs of water are bursting through like an oasis in the middle of desolation. Watch for it…you will see it…it will surprise and free you.

FROM ISAIAH 43:18–19

WARRANTY NOTES: ISN'T GOD AMAZING? ONLY HE REDEEMS OUR PAST AND TURNS IT INTO SOMETHING GOOD.

Dear God, thank You for reminding me that I don't have to dwell on what has already happened. I choose to concentrate on now and notice the good You are doing, even in the midst of dry spells and confusion. Thank You, Lord, for doing a new thing in me.
Amen.

God Guarantees

I HAVE PLANS TO PROSPER YOUR CHILD

I created each of your child's days. That means I have thoughts and plans for them. And My plans will never be for evil—to harm or hurt; they will only be to bring about good in their lives. I have designed a hopeful future, and your kids' welfare is always uppermost in My mind. The final outcome will be peace and well-being.

FROM JEREMIAH 29:10–11

WARRANTY NOTES: GOD HAS A FAULTLESS BLUEPRINT FOR A FLAWLESS RESULT.

Dear God,
When negative things happen,
I'm sometimes tempted to blame You. Forgive me.
I am reminded today that You
have plans for my child—plans for good!
I leave his/her future in Your hands.
Amen.

God Guarantees

I WILL TELL YOU WHAT YOU NEED TO KNOW

Mother, daughter, child of Mine, call on Me when you don't know what to do. I know that many things in parenting and in life are hidden and hard to understand. I promise to respond to your call and give you the answers you need. There are so many great and glorious things that you do not know—yet. You can spend your whole lifetime finding out all that I want to reveal to you.

FROM JEREMIAH 33:3

WARRANTY NOTES: WE DON'T HAVE TO KNOW EVERYTHING, BECAUSE GOD ALREADY DOES.

Dear God, instinctively I know that I cannot be a good mother without You. You are only a "call" away and You promise to answer. I pray You'll help me call on You to discover all the wonderful things You have for me to know about being a mom.

Amen.

God Guarantees

No One Will Make You or Your Child Afraid

My promise is to bring peace to your land. Your "land" is your territory, your home, your place of living. I will keep the beasts of loss and destruction from destroying your domain. You and your family can lay your heads on your pillows at night, knowing peaceful sleep and freedom from fear.

FROM LEVITICUS 26:6

WARRANTY NOTES: THE "MONSTERS" OF THIS WORLD MAY BE FOR REAL, BUT OUR FEAR NEEDN'T BE.

Dear God,
Thank You, God, that we need never know real fear
because You are our protector and deliverer in every area
of our lives. My child and I will sleep restfully tonight
because we confidently entrust our cares to You.
Amen.

Multnomah Publishers

The publisher and author would love to hear your
comments about this book. *Please contact us at:*
www.multnomah.net/guarantees

An Unlimited Partnership

God. Man. Woman. A three-party agreement built to last. The fine print of these lifetime Warranty Notes sets forth God's eternal covenant with husbands and wives and assures His unfailing commitment to your future together. Find key promises on finances, fidelity, forgiveness, faith, and more. Carry them. Share them. Build on them securely. Signed, sealed, delivered—they're yours!

ISBN 1-59052-022-X

FOR WIVES WHO STAY…EVEN WHEN IT HURTS.

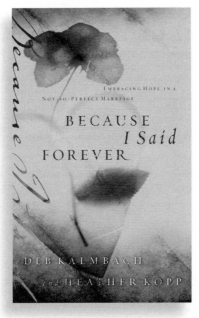

Maybe you feel a little jaded. You've read Christian marriage books but can't identify. The problems seem trivial, the solutions unrealistic. This book is different. Guided by scriptural principles, the authors provide life-tested advice and solid spiritual support for a wife making the tough choice to stay in a difficult marriage. It will help you find wisdom in nurturing your marriage, patience in honoring your husband, and the courage to keep reaching for God's best each day.

ISBN 1-57673-852-3